SKETCHES IN COLOR

SETS ONE AND TWO FOR PIANO SOLO

BY ROBERT STARER
EDITED BY CAROLYN TRUE

To access companion recorded performances online, visit:
www.halleonard.com/mylibrary

6602-5198-7043-8158

ISBN 978-1-4234-1519-0

HAL•LEONARD®
CORPORATION
7777 W. BLUEMOUND RD. P.O. BOX 13819 MILWAUKEE, WI 53213

Visit Hal Leonard Online at
www.halleonard.com

EDITORIAL PREFACE

I have always considered myself a lucky pianist. I have had wonderful teachers from the beginning, starting with my mother, Marilyn True. From my first lesson until I graduated from high school, Mom fostered in me a love of music, pianos and pianists, and an appreciation for fine artistry. She taught me to understand and interpret each musical score, identifying the structure and function of each sonority. Communication, passion, and beauty were the most important facets of any performance. My father, Wesley True, was my second teacher, inspiring me to delve into each score, investigating all musical options. He refined my understanding of interpretation and challenged me to think critically and listen actively. Between the two of them, they taught me for 18 years, and frankly, I have never stopped learning from them.

One of the greatest gifts my parents gave me was a concerted love, respect, and curiosity for contemporary music. Dad was a musical rebel in Missouri–performing and teaching new, cutting-edge pieces almost every time he graced a stage. Mom assigned pieces that were appropriate for my age and level, and at the same time were new and exciting. By the time I was eleven, I had played music composed by Ross Lee Finney, Anton Webern, Béla Bartók, and Robert Starer, to name a few.

The first time I heard *Bright Orange* I thought it was the most thrilling piece I had ever heard. I couldn't wait to play it! And the rest of the set–who could resist the tenderness of *Pink*, the laid-back cool of *Shades of Blue*, the atmosphere of *Grey*, or the explosive energy of *Crimson*?

Starer's **Sketches in Color** have remained some of my favorite pieces, and to have the opportunity to work with both volumes has been a joy. Within this edition are fourteen outstanding piano pieces full of color and beauty. Every student will find at least one piece that is their next "favorite." I hope you and your students will explore these pieces, play them, and love them as I have.

—Carolyn True

ABOUT THE EDITOR

Hailed as "an artist with commanding technique, always at the service of the music and capable of taming any tigers the composer has unleashed" (Windeler, *San Antonio Express News*), Carolyn True is a pianist equally at home on the concert stage and in the teaching studio. A member of the music faculty of Trinity University, True teaches individual lessons, accompanying, piano ensemble, piano literature, piano pedagogy, and other related courses. She walks the delicate balance between teaching in San Antonio, giving workshops, master classes, seminars, and adjudicating and actively performing as soloist and chamber musician in the United States, Europe, and Asia. A compassionate and challenging professor, True is carrying on the family tradition. In 2000, True was recognized as the Texas Music Teachers Association's Collegiate Teacher of the Year.

Dr. True holds the prestigious Performer's Certificate and the D.M.A. degree from the Eastman School of Music, an M.M. from the University of Maryland-College Park, and the B.M. from the University of Central Missouri and was a prize winner in national and international competitions. She was also the recipient of a Rotary Foundation Scholarship for study at the Conservatoire National de la Musique in Lyon, France.

Her first solo CD, *Carolyn True 1*, features works of Ligeti, Bach/Brahms, Beethoven, and Bennett.

ROBERT STARER BIOGRAPHY

The composer Robert Starer (January 8, 1924 – April 22, 2001) was born in Vienna, the son of a textile factory owner. As a young child he was raised primarily by household help, but later on a French governess was hired who soon discovered Starer's perfect pitch. Although later he was to remark that perfect pitch is no great help to a musician, the governess thought it was a wonderful parlor trick to show off to important visitors. When he was four, the family hired a sour teacher named Köppel to begin Robert's piano instruction. Starer disliked lessons and in particular practicing, because he practiced by mindlessly repeating passages. He found klimpern (doodling) much more enjoyable and would regularly put a book on the music rack and read and doodle while he was supposed to be working. He remembered, "Luckily for me my mother, in the next room, could not tell whether I was improvising–a word I did not know then–or practicing, and as long as sounds came from the piano she was satisfied." He entered the Vienna State Conservatory in 1937 and studied with Victor Ebenstein. Shortly after the Germans annexed Austria, a uniformed man came to the conservatory and into Ebenstein's classroom and ordered all Jewish or part Jewish students to leave. Soon after, Starer was sent out of Vienna by his parents. He took the trip to Jerusalem by himself and was never to see his mother again.

Starer attended the Jerusalem Conservatory (1938-1943) where he studied both piano and composition with Josef Tal. The progression from pianist to composer was aided by a chance encounter. Starer was practicing, or more exactly, "doodling" at the piano. Tal heard the sounds Starer was making, and entering the room, asked to hear them again. Starer replied that he had no idea what he had just played, because he was making it up. Tal told him to play more, but to always write down what he was doing. Tal suggested that he was to "write down only those ideas that deserved to be retained and had a memorable quality... and then work hard to give that idea the best possible shape before trying to develop it." This directive set Starer on his path as a composer.

In 1943 Starer joined the British Royal Air Force, serving for three years. He then moved to the United States and resumed his musical studies at the Juilliard School with Jacobi and at Tanglewood with Copland. Shortly after receiving a post-graduate diploma from Juilliard, Starer became a member of the faculty. Teaching was an essential part of Starer's life. According to him, composition students can be broken into two categories–those who look inside for inspiration, and those who look outside themselves for models to imitate. The latter is easy–students will come to a lesson with pieces that sound reminiscent of other composers. The former category is the most difficult, for by looking inward, one must take risks, sometimes successfully sometimes unsuccessfully. The end result however, is an individual communicative voice. Starer joined the faculties of the Juilliard School (1949-1974) and Brooklyn College CUNY (1963-1991). In addition to teaching, he wrote two rhythmic studies, **Basic Rhythm Training** and **Rhythm Training**, that are used in many music schools to this day.

PERFORMANCE NOTES

MUSICAL CHARACTERISTICS

Starer's musical language was primarily traditional, but he experimented throughout his life with serialism, chance music, and other 20th century compositional techniques. Starer believed his music was composed of "elements of Viennese sentiment, Jewish melisma, Near Eastern playfulness and American jazz." Although Starer did not teach many younger students, he did study them and their music making, in particular while his son Dan was growing up. The first volume of *Sketches in Color* was composed after listening and watching Dan begin piano lessons. Starer believed in the accuracy of children's perceptions and refused to condescend, bore, or overwhelm them with bombast. He limited himself only with awareness of hand size, technical endurance, and compositional complexity. The first volume of *Sketches in Color* was written in 1963, the second in 1973.

PEDALING

When pedaling, several issues need to be addressed, including, but certainly not limited to: the character of the piece, the color of the desired sound, the dryness or wetness of the sound, the carry-over of harmonies and/or melodic notes, and the function of rests, fermatas, and other durational indications. Too often, pianists simply "put down the right foot" and take it off when the moment strikes them. They need to be aware of the variety of sounds possible by choosing to pedal carefully. There is ample opportunity in these pieces to experiment with various levels of damper and una corda pedals, and even a few moments where one could use the sostenuto pedal for clarity.

The pedal indications used in this edition are:

1) **damper pedal** – (⌐_____∧_____, 1/2⌐_____⌐, *flutter ped.* ⌐)

Experiment with the depths of pedal by watching the dampers raise while slowly depressing the pedal. It is simplest to play a series of chords or a set of random single pitches. Listen to the sounds produced by depressing the pedal all of the way, halfway, and a quarter of the way down. Flutter pedaling is a little trickier, but can be a pianist's greatest tool. While playing the same series of chords or pitches as before, experience flutter pedaling by rapidly yet subtly moving the pedal up and down.

2) **una corda pedal** – (*u.c.*)

Depress the U.C. slowly while watching the hammers shift. Depending on the age and type of piano, the shift will result in hammers striking the strings with either softer or harder felts. By adjusting the depth of the U.C. one can determine the amount of hammer shift. Each place on the hammer will drastically change the sound of the pitch. For example, if, when using the U.C., the hammers shift to strike the strings with deeply grooved felt (a harder felt surface), the sound will be edgier, even tinny.

3) **sostenuto pedal** – (*sost.*)

Many pianists wait years to explore the sostenuto pedal on a grand piano. One need not be afraid of using this tool. Its use can greatly clarify a thick texture by sustaining a few pitches, allowing others to remain dryer and more articulate. Play the lowest pitch on the piano and hold it. Depress the sostenuto pedal to capture the damper in its raised position. Let go of the key, but keep the pedal depressed. Now play random pitches all over the keyboard. Listen to the resultant sounds of harmonics from the original pitch and the clarity of the pitches not held by the sostenuto pedal. Experiment with adding a bit of damper pedal to the random sounds.

FINGERING

Fingering is as individual as hands are different. When choosing fingerings, one needs to address the desires of the composer (length and dynamic of note patterns, articulation, other expressive elements), phrasing, geography of the keyboard, and natural and efficient physical motions produced by understanding the parameters of the individual hand–length of fingers, breadth of expanse, girth of the fingers and the palm. There are traditional fingerings that serve most hands (for example, a B Major scale fingering) and many others that serve one hand extraordinarily well while failing another's hand miserably. The fingerings for this edition are merely suggestions (the editor's are in italics, the composer's are in normal text). As with pedaling, pianists must spend time exploring fingering options and coming to a conscious decision for each passage. In this way, the musical goals will always be first and foremost.

PRACTICE AND PERFORMANCE SUGGESTIONS

In his preface to the first Volume of *Sketches in Color*, Starer writes, "*Sketches in Color* are intended for study as well as for performance. The titles are obviously rather personal, since associations between sounds and colors are arbitrary at best. The pieces employ different 20th century techniques to create their different moods." Starer started the compositional process by clearly imagining each color and its properties, and followed by matching the color in his mind's eye with musical sounds. In many of the pieces in both volumes, Starer uses a variety of textures to depict different hues and shadings. One must define each texture's sonority, technical challenge, and place within the larger section of the piece to communicate all of the facets of color.

. . . .

SKETCHES IN COLOR, SET I

1. PURPLE

According to Starer, purple is "a rich color, perhaps a little murky at times." The musical richness is due to polytonality (two different keys functioning simultaneously). In *Purple*, Starer mixes first inversion and root position triads with open fifths and fourths. For example, in m.1 there are E♭ Major first inversion triads in the right hand while the left hand has E natural and B natural. Identify the two implied tonalities every time there are chords. Experiment with each polytonal section by shifting one hand or the other to produce the same key (for example, in m.1 play an E♭ perfect fifth in the left hand and leave the right hand as is). Listen to hear the difference between polytonality and traditional diatonic writing. In *Purple*, polytonality alternates with monophonic melodies doubled three octaves apart. Carefully balance the two voices equally.

2. SHADES OF BLUE

There are several "shades of blue" one can see–bright, blue sky, the blue of the ocean, a deep cobalt blue of Mexican tiles, to name only three–and the musical shades of the blues tinged with sadness. In Starer's *Shades of Blue*, the right hand melody is touched by accidentals, including "blue notes" that bend the tonality (example – m.1 E-natural turns into E♭). The left hand progresses slowly but inexorably up the keyboard with perfect fifths. Take a little time, but not too much, before the return of the opening motive. Notice the change of dynamics between the first measure and the return at m. 21.

3. BLACK AND WHITE

The title refers to the black and white keys on the keyboard. When one plays only the black keys, they produce the five pitches of a pentatonic scale. When playing only the white keys, they produce a C Major scale. In this piece, one plays the two tonalities at the same time, resulting in new and colorful sounds. Notice that each staff has a different key signature and that they switch back and forth. (Starer reported that when he sent the manuscript to the engravers, he was questioned about the "crazy key signatures.") Careful pedaling is necessary to retain the legato melody while producing an impressionistic atmosphere with the rolling accompaniment pattern. Experiment with different lengths and levels of pedal to find the most beautiful sounds. By changing fingers on the repeated notes one can keep the fleshy part of the fingers on the key, producing a warmer sound. (Using the same finger on repeated notes, the attack is much faster and direct. The sound will be more angular and cold and less appropriate for this piece.)

4. BRIGHT ORANGE

Representing one of the brightest and most vivid colors of the rainbow, this is one of the fastest, most animated pieces of the set. Practice with the metronome to retain steadiness, to avoid rushing faster than the indication, and to point out the syncopations. The syncopations in the accompaniment and the short, angular units in the melody contribute to the brilliance. As with *Shades of Blue*, Starer uses "blue notes" to give *Bright Orange* a jazzy feel.

5. GREY

Grey is like the color–an impression without a vivid central color. To musically reflect this lack of center, Starer chose to use a 12- tone row rather than a diatonic scale (a set order of all 12 different pitches is called a row). This row can be manipulated by playing the pitches in the original order (the 12-tone series or row), backwards (inversion), upside down (retrograde), or upside down and backward (retrograde inversion). In *Grey*, Starer marked each appearance of the row in the score wherever and however it appeared (S = 12-tone series, I = Inversion, R = Retrograde, RI = Retrograde Inversion). Between statements of the row he divided the twelve pitches three different ways–mm. 1-2 into two groups of six (two whole-tone scales), mm. 7-8 into clusters and diminished triads, and mm.14-15 into quartal chords (chords built of fourths instead of thirds). The dynamics for *Grey* are low and subtle. Listen to the color of each compositional technique used and enjoy the variety of sonorities.

6. PINK

The slowest and most sentimental of the pieces in Volume I, *Pink* is a delicate piece with a tuneful melody that spins itself out effortlessly between 3/4 and 2/4 meters. Keep feeling the quarter note pulse and the changes will be subtle and easy. The opening motive (m. 1) recurs with several transpositions (mm. 10, 13, and 14). As with most piano melodies, the key to this piece is to literally sing the line. Sing it aloud to see how one would naturally shape the melody. Rather than treating the pulse metronomically, be free to give and take. Think of the time as a rubber band. There will be moments of moving slightly ahead or taking a little bit of time; the band can be stretched, but not too far or it will break. Above all the rubber band needs to always return home to retain its shape. Starer said that the color pink reminded him of youngsters–hopeful and pretty–beautifully demonstrated in this piece.

7. CRIMSON

Crimson is a strong color and in Starer's piece the speed, percussive quality of the repeated-note accompaniment, and the angular rhythm of the melody are perfectly evocative. Opening and ending with a single-line fanfare, *Crimson* is an energetic romp in 7/8. Keep the right wrist supple as it quickly repeats one, two, and finally three pitches. Remember the gesture of dribbling a basketball–drop the ball, follow through the motion with the wrist, and allow the ball and wrist to bounce back up comfortably and naturally–and adjust this motion to the piano. Drop into each pitch, follow through to the bottom of the key for a full sound, and bounce back up to the starting position. In particular, check to keep the thumb and fifth finger relaxed.

· · · · · · · · · · · · · · ·

SKETCHES IN COLOR, SET 2

1. MAROON

In *Maroon*, Starer alternates between pedaled ringing chords and clusters with fast-moving sixteenth notes. Practice the first four measures to explore different types of sound productions noting articulation marks, dynamics and lengths. The sixteenth-note passages (mm. 5 – 8 and mm. 14 – 15) need fluidity and clean articulation to be heard through the composer's pedal indications. The editor has suggested ½ pedals for clarity. Practice the contrary motion passages with different rhythm patterns for absolute accuracy of ear and finger.

2. ALUMINUM

A bright and shiny, metallic color, Starer's *Aluminum* is full of fast-paced staccato notes and interruptive, blocked intervals. Staccato is not a rhythmic value, but an articulation–play the notes detached and lively. It is very tempting to play this piece loud and fast, but Starer left specific indications that beautifully show the architectural shape. Grade the dynamics (from *pp* in m. 49 to *ff* in m. 22) and the shape will be communicated.

3. SILVER AND GOLD

In Starer's setting of *Silver and Gold*, each hand may represent one of the two precious metals. The left hand has a 12-note ostinato pattern (mm. 1 – 6) that repeats without change from the beginning to the end of the piece. This inexorable pattern sets a steady pulse and works as the foundation for the singing "espressivo" melody of the right hand. Be careful, however, to keep the left hand at a constant *p* dynamic, unfazed by the right hand singing. The melody shifts the subdivision of the beat from duple, to triple, to quadruple, so the steadiness of the left hand is imperative. The three-note unit, d-e-f, pervades the melody which expands both by interval and register and then contracts to end the piece on d.

4. KHAKI

Starer begins *Khaki* with a pianist's snare drum cadence. Make sure the left hand grace notes move quickly, cleanly, and lightly into the right hand clusters. The cadence (mm. 1 – 3) is marked *p*, as heard from a distance. It recurs three times (mm. 1 - 3, mm. 8 – 11, and mm. 17 – 19) almost identically; in the middle statement, Starer varies the left hand slightly (m. 9 and m. 11). Alternating between the drum rolls are militaristic, angular melodies which stop and start abruptly. Executing this piece with rhythmic precision will make *Khaki* march along.

5. PEPPER AND SALT

This spicy piece is exciting to play! Starer uses clusters in each hand to punctuate, to accompany, and to suspend. Carefully balance the clusters dependent on their function; for example, m. 3 is accompanimental and could be balanced rather evenly between the voices, m. 9 is climactic, brilliant, and uses the highest pitch of the piece, m. 13 serves as a moment of suspense. Experiement with different voicings to change the flavor (voice high, voice evenly, voice low). In addition to clusters, Starer has two other textures–repeated single notes (F4 in m. 2, B3 in m. 3, or E2 in m. 8) and pitches sprinkled out in contrary motion from the middle of the keyboard to the extremities and back (example m. 1). Keep the repeated notes beautiful yet precise (the editor has suggested using one finger per repeated note set). Practice the "sprinkled" sections hands alone for ease and for consistency of line. Then put the hands together to hear the dialogue between the hands. The use of the sostenuto pedal in m. 17 allows for both the cluster's sonority to be held and the repeated notes to sound staccato.

6. AQUAMARINE

This jazzy piece has a flowing melody in the right hand supported by a quarter-note ostinato in the left hand (the ostinato is complete in the first measure). Notice the difference of meters for each hand. Although each has five main pulses, the subdivisions are slightly different (three subdivisions in the right hand, two in the left). Starer uses "blue notes" to color both the melody and the three-note chords. Play the right hand articulations with a flowing legato and lifts at the end of almost every unit.

7. CHROME YELLOW

As Starer marks, *Chrome Yellow* is to be played, "not too fast, quite brittle." It is bright, extremely active and reminiscent of Bartók. Notice the macro- and micro-phrases extending and shortening rhythmic units. The left hand has a jumpy melody while the right hand has active clusters. The meter shifts quickly and often from 3/8 to 2/4 to 5/8, but as with other pieces in this set, has a constant eighth-note pulse. Practice playing the rhythm on a tabletop or the key cover for accuracy. Then practice with the correct pitches on the keyboard and listen to the excitement grow!

RESOURCES

Ayesh, Kevin Bradley. The Solo Piano Music of Robert Starer. DMA paper College Park: University of Maryland, 1990 113 p. UM 9121463.

Starer, Robert. Continuo. New York: Random House, 1987.

PREFACE (SET ONE)

SKETCHES IN COLOR (Seven Pieces for Piano) are intended for study as well as for performance. The titles are obviously rather personal, since associations between sounds and colors are arbitrary at best.

The pieces employ different 20th century techniques to create their different moods:

1. PURPLE uses polytonality (triads against fourths and fifths).

2. SHADES OF BLUE has diatonic melody versus chromatic, to the accompaniment of parallel fifths.

3. BLACK AND WHITE juxtaposes the pentatonic scale of the black keys to the diatonic scale of the white keys, alternating between the hands.

4. BRIGHT ORANGE employs parallel harmony and jazz syncopation.

5. GREY uses the four basic forms of a 12-tone row: The row or series itself, its inversion, retrograde and retrograde inversion. In the measures in which the row does not appear, the chords are constructed to include all 12 tones in every bar or every two bars.

6. PINK is very tonal, especially in the sense that it uses modulation, or rather the sudden shifting of tonal centers, as a structural principle.

7. CRIMSON uses different rhythmic divisions of a constant 7/8 meter.

In performance not all seven pieces have to be played together, nor do they have to appear in the sequence in which they are published. They may also be performed without their titles.

Robert Starer

1. Purple

By Robert Starer

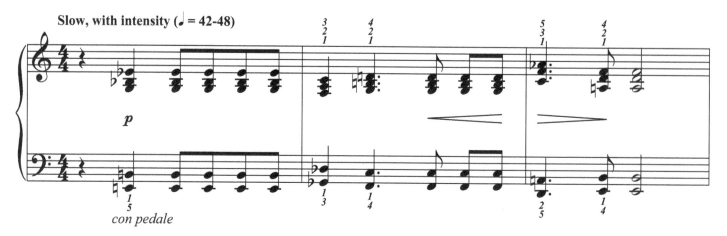

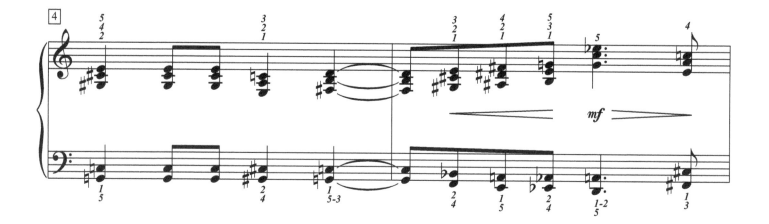

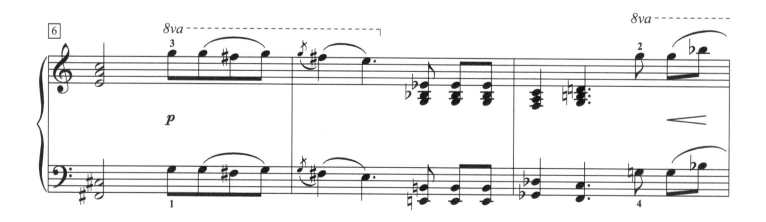

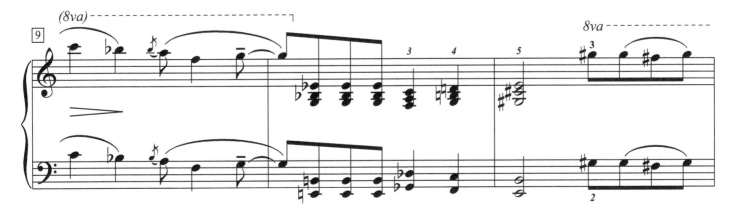

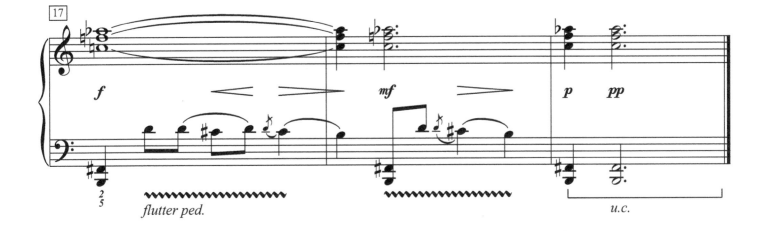

2. Shades of Blue

By Robert Starer

3. Black and White

By Robert Starer

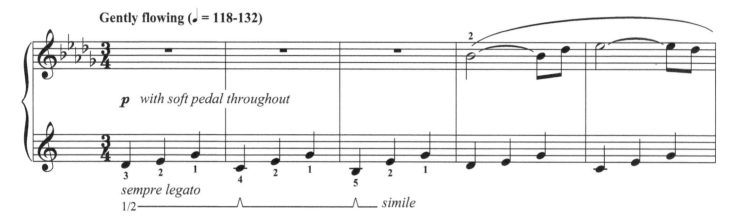

4. Bright Orange

By Robert Starer

Fast and light (♩ = 152)

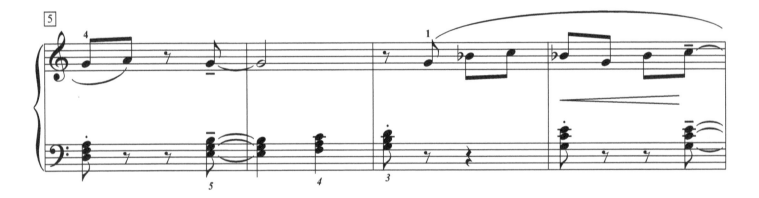

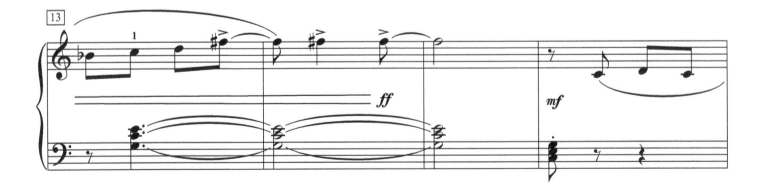

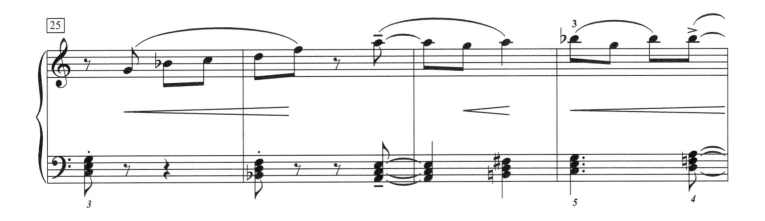

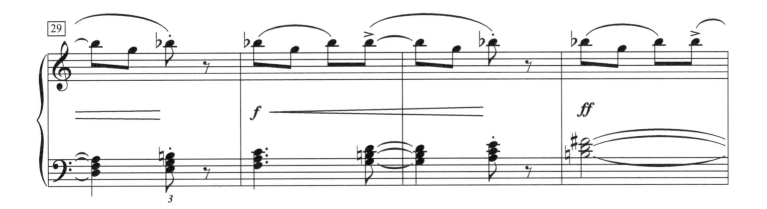

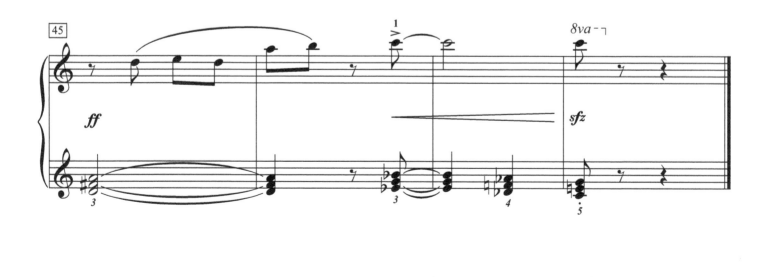

5. Grey

S = 12 tone series   **I** = Inversion   **R** = Retrograde   **RI** = Retrograde Inversions

By Robert Starer

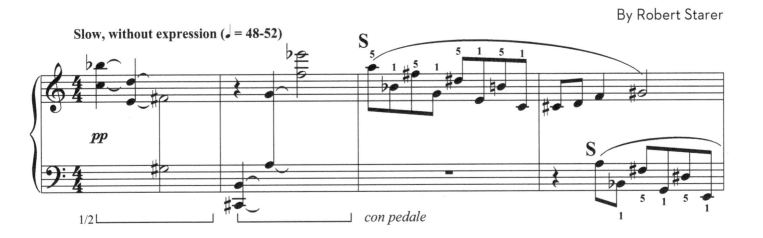

6. Pink

By Robert Starer

Not too fast, with sentiment (♩ = 54-60)

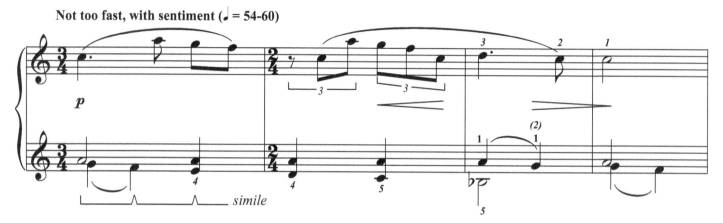

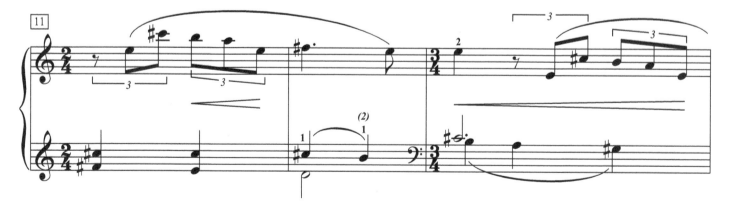

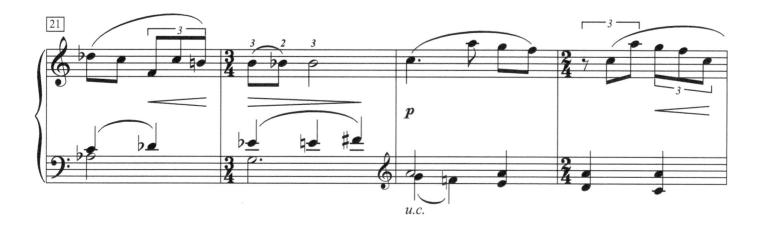

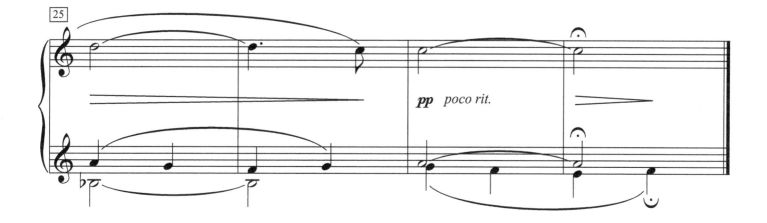

7. Crimson

By Robert Starer

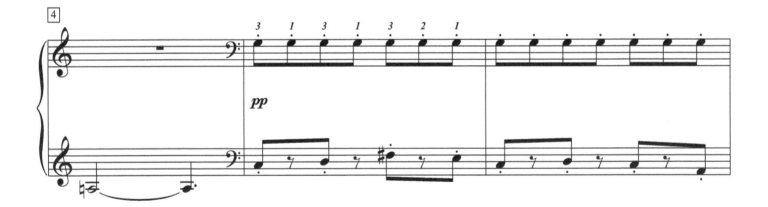

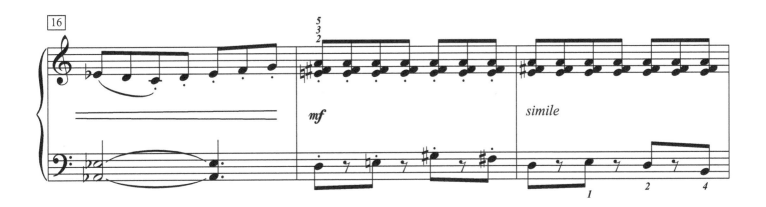

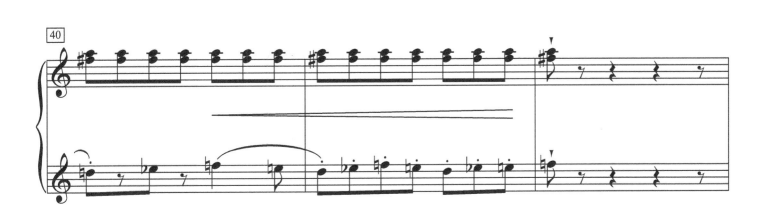

PREFACE (SET TWO)

SKETCHES IN COLOR (Seven Pieces for Piano) Set Two, are more advanced than Set One, both in the demands they make on the player and in the compositional techniques employed.

1. MAROON has no melody, little rhythm; it is almost pure color. Careful attention to dynamics and pedaling will bring out its true shade.

2. ALUMINUM combines added-note chords in parallel motion with polytonality.

3. SILVER AND GOLD – "**Silver**", the ostinato accompaniment in the left hand, constantly repeats its twelve notes, like a row. "**Gold**" is threaded against it, with D as a tonal center; a point of departure and of return.

4. KHAKI is the color of a soldier's uniform, the color of drum rolls, of bugles and fifes.

5. PEPPER AND SALT has symmetrically-built chords (chords of identical intervals) and a variety of clusters in half-tone and whole-tone combinations.

6. AQUAMARINE suggests "blues," although it is in quintuple time.

7. CRIMSON is mostly concerned with rhythm. It has non-symmetrical rhythms set in symmetrically-shaped phrases.

As in Set One, these pieces do not have to be played together or in the order in which they appear. They may be performed without their titles.

Robert Starer

1. Maroon

By Robert Starer

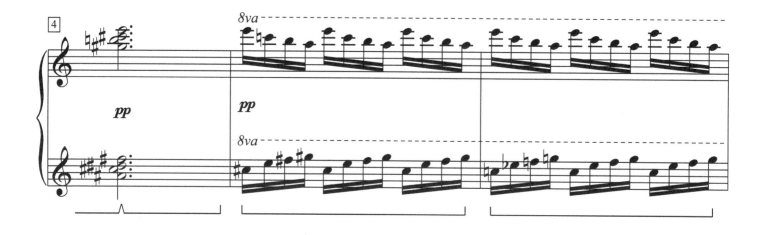

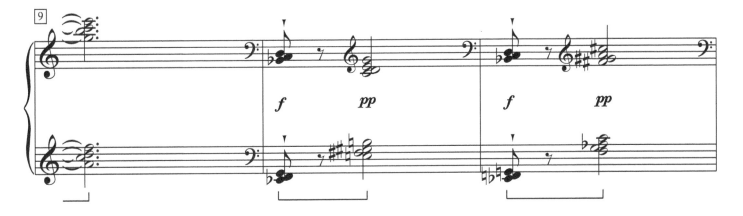

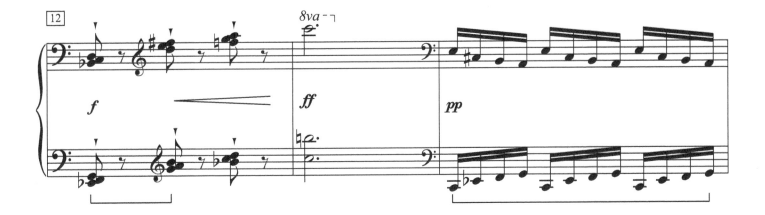

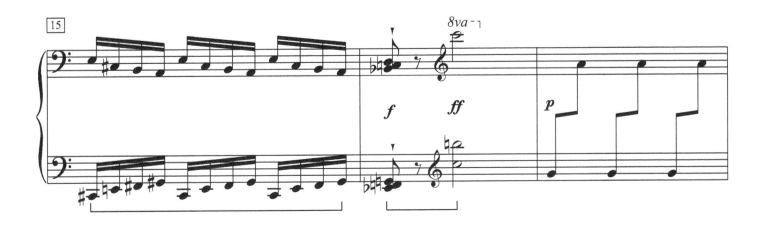

2. Aluminum

By Robert Starer

Fast and even (♩ = 152-160)

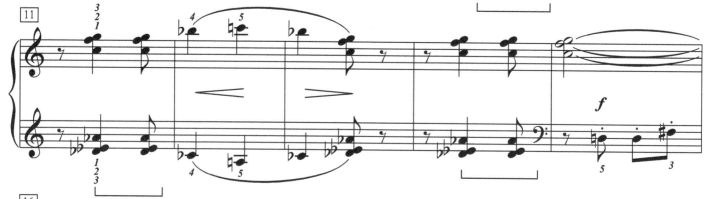

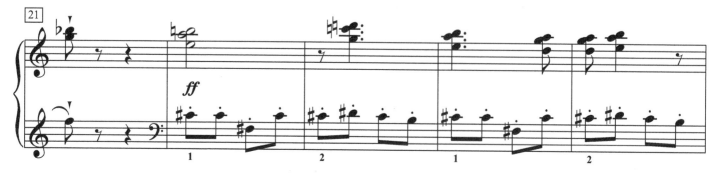

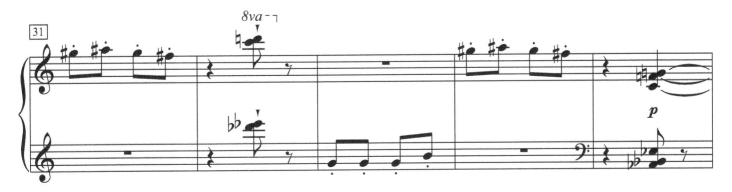

3. Silver and Gold

By Robert Starer

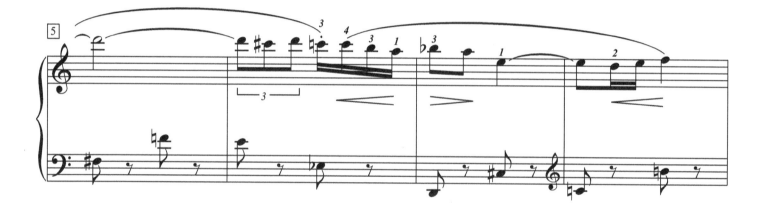

4. Khaki

By Robert Starer

In march-time (♩ = 120)

(For color contrast use u.c. for soft passages)

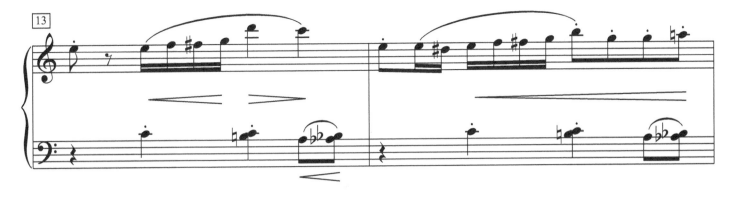

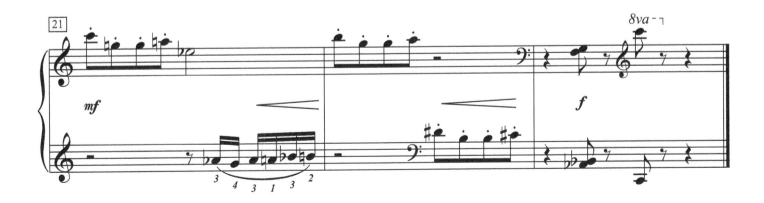

5. Pepper and Salt

By Robert Starer

Fast and light (♩ = 139-160)

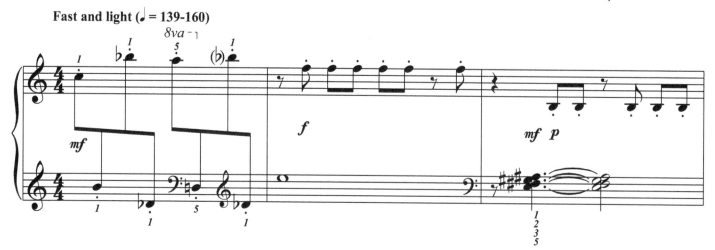

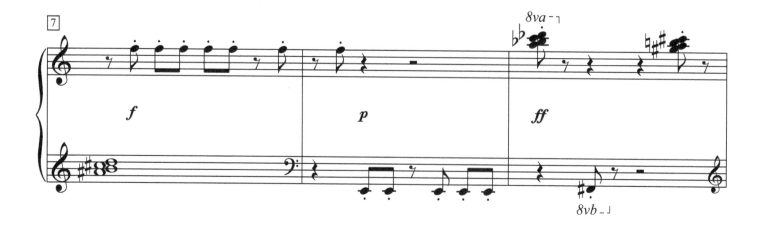

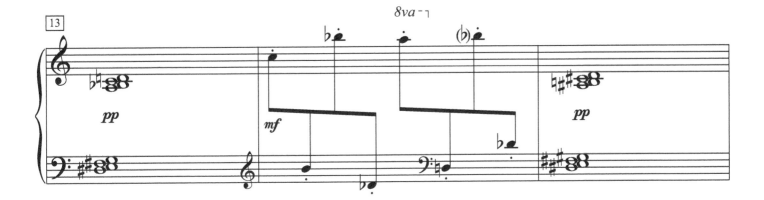

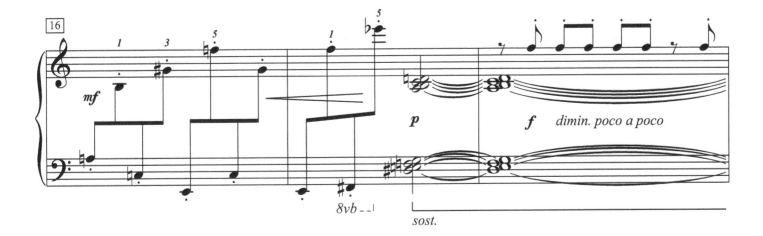

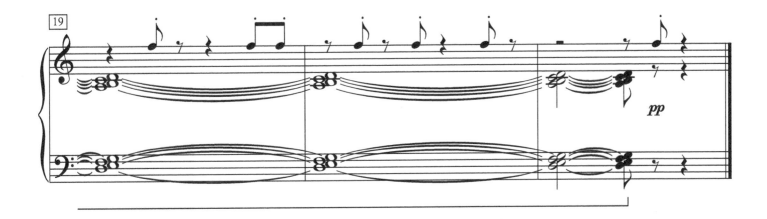

6. Aquamarine

By Robert Starer

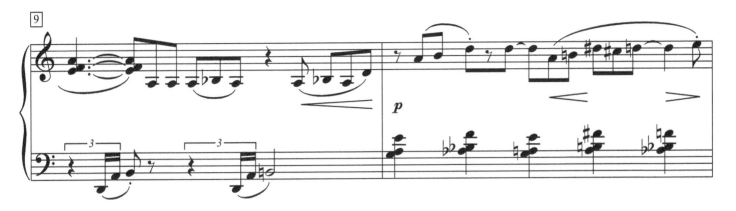

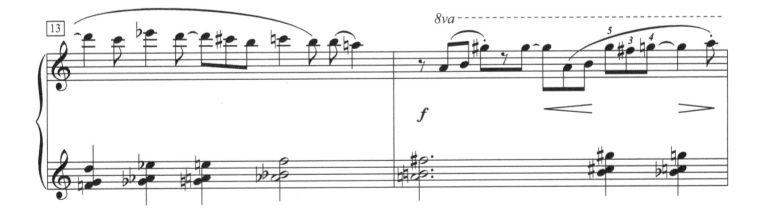

7. Chrome Yellow

By Robert Starer

Not too fast, quite brittle (♩ = 144-160)

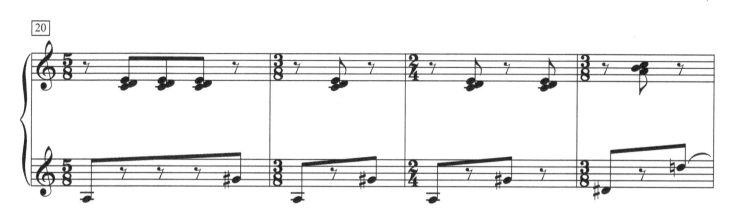

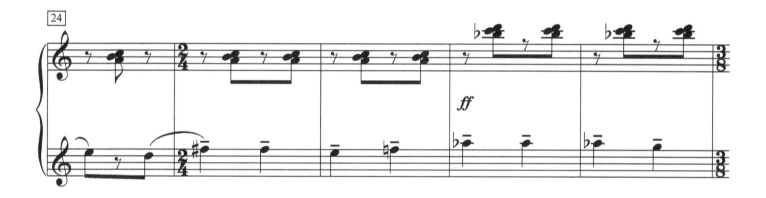

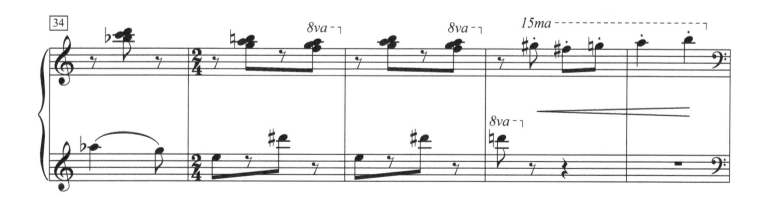

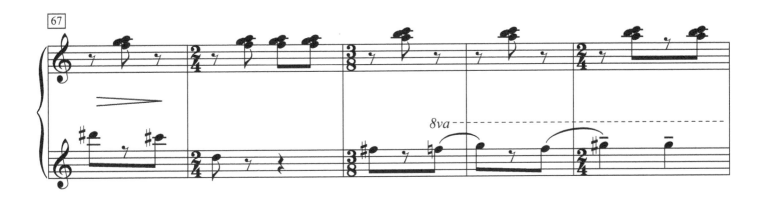

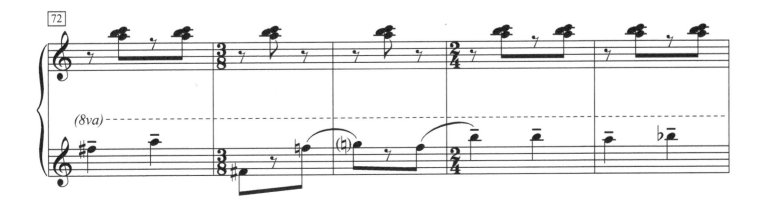

SKETCHES IN COLOR, SET 1

	PURPLE	SHADES OF BLUE	BLACK AND WHITE	BRIGHT ORANGE	GREY	PINK	CRIMSON
Level	6	5	5	6	6	6	7
Suggested Teaching Order	3	1	2	4	6	5	7
Key	Polytonal	C Major	Polytonal; 2 different key signatures	C Major	12-Tone	F Major	Chromatic with C as tonic
Number of measures	19	20	42	48	18	28	46
Meter	4/4	6/8	3/4	2/4	4/4	3/4, 2/4	7/8
Tempo	♩=48	♩.=80	♩=132	♩=152	♩=52	♩=60	♩=184
Dynamic range	*pp* – *f*	*p* – *f*	*pp* – *mf*	*mf* – *ff*	*ppp* – *p*	*pp* – *poco f*	*pp* – *ff*
Pitch range	B1 – C#7	F2 – B6	E3 – E♭6	A1 – C7	G#1 – A7	E♭3 – A5	C1 – G#6
Greatest span	sixth	octave	sixth	fifth	seventh	seventh	fifth
Number of voices	5	3	Primarily 2, later four (3 tied in left hand, 1 in right hand)	4	6	3	3
Challenge elements	Careful pedaling; two contrasting textures (chordal, mono-phonic)	Steadiness; syncopations	Maneuvering positions on black and white keys	Jazzy rhythms	Singing atonal lines within very soft volumes	Steadiness of the quarter note beat; different subdivisions (duple, triple, quadruple)	Bouncy repeated figures; avoiding wrist and forearm tension

SKETCHES IN COLOR, SET 2

	MAROON	ALUMINUM	SILVER AND GOLD	KHAKI	PEPPER AND SALT	AQUAMARINE	CHROME YELLOW
Level	7	8	7	7	8	7	8
Suggested Teaching Order	4	5	3	1	6	2	7
Key	C tonic	experimental	12-tone ostinato bass	C tonic	experimental	experimental	C tonic
Number of measures	20	50	32	23	21	16	97
Meter	3/4	2/4	2/4	4/4	4/4	15/8 right hand 5/4 left hand	2/4, 3/8, 5/8
Tempo	♩=60-62	♩=152-160	♩=58	♩=120	♩=138-144	♩=76	♩=144-152
Dynamic range	pp – ff	pp – ff	pp – f	pp – f	pp – ff	pp – f	mf – ff
Pitch range	C1-C7	A♭1-E6	D1-B♭6	F#1-C7	F#1-D♭7	D1-B6	F#1-D7
Greatest span	seventh	fifth	seventh	fifth	seventh	octave	seventh
Number of voices	8	6	2	4 (cluster)	9 (clusters + 1)	4	4 (single vs 3)
Challenge elements	Slow pulse; careful pedaling	Fast position shifts; rhythmic challenges	Steadiness and sempre p left hand; expressive atonal melody	Position shifts; rapid grace note figures	Extreme jumping; fast position shifts	Jazz rhythms; unusual but consistent metric indications (in 5)	Rapid changes of meter; quick position shifts